Acting Edition

Shadow Play

A Musical Fantasy

from
Tonight at 8:30

by Noël Coward

Copyright © 1935 by Noël Coward
Copyright © 1936 in *Tonight at 8:30* by Noël Coward
Copyright © 1938 (Acting Edition) by Noël Coward
Copyright © 1962, 1963, 1965 (in renewal) by Noël Coward
All Rights Reserved

SHADOW PLAY is fully protected under the copyright laws of the United States of America, the British Commonwealth, including Canada, and all member countries of the Berne Convention for the Protection of Literary and Artistic Works, the Universal Copyright Convention, and/or the World Trade Organization conforming to the Agreement on Trade Related Aspects of Intellectual Property Rights. All rights, including professional and amateur stage productions, recitation, lecturing, public reading, motion picture, radio broadcasting, television, online/digital production, and the rights of translation into foreign languages are strictly reserved.

ISBN 978-0-573-62462-9

www.concordtheatricals.com
www.concordtheatricals.co.uk

FOR PRODUCTION INQUIRIES

UNITED STATES AND CANADA
info@concordtheatricals.com
1-866-979-0447

UNITED KINGDOM AND EUROPE
licensing@concordtheatricals.co.uk
020-7054-7298

Each title is subject to availability from Concord Theatricals Corp., depending upon country of performance. Please be aware that *SHADOW PLAY* may not be licensed by Concord Theatricals Corp. in your territory. Professional and amateur producers should contact the nearest Concord Theatricals Corp. office or licensing partner to verify availability.

CAUTION: Professional and amateur producers are hereby warned that *SHADOW PLAY* is subject to a licensing fee. The purchase, renting, lending or use of this book does not constitute a license to perform this title(s), which license must be obtained from Concord Theatricals Corp. prior to any performance. Performance of this title(s) without a license is a violation of federal law and may subject the producer and/or presenter of such performances to civil penalties. Both amateurs and professionals considering a production are strongly advised to apply to the appropriate agent before starting rehearsals, advertising, or booking a theatre. A licensing fee must be paid whether the title(s) is presented for charity or gain and whether or not admission is charged. Professional/Stock licensing fees are quoted upon application to Concord Theatricals Corp.

Please refer to page 42 for further copyright information.

SHADOW PLAY

SHADOW PLAY

Produced by John C. Wilson at the National Theatre in New York City on November 27, 1936, as one of a series of nine one-act plays by Noel Coward, under the title of "TO-NIGHT AT EIGHT-THIRTY." The play was directed by the author and the cast was as follows:

VICTORIA GAYFORTH	*Gertrude Lawrence.*
SIMON GAYFORTH	*Noel Coward.*
MARTHA CUNNINGHAM	*Joyce Carey.*
HODGE	*Kenneth Carten.*
A YOUNG MAN	*Anthony Pelissier.*
GEORGE CUNNINGHAM	*Alan Webb.*
LENA	*Moya Nugent.*
SIBYL HESTON	*Joan Swinstead.*
MICHAEL DOYLE	*Edward Underdown.*

TIME.—The Present.

SHADOW PLAY

First produced at the Opera House, Manchester, and subsequently at the Phoenix Theatre, Charing Cross Road, London, W.C.2., in January, 1936, with the following cast of characters:

VICTORIA GAYFORTH	*Gertrude Lawrence.*
SIMON GAYFORTH	*Noel Coward.*
MARTHA CUNNINGHAM	*Everley Gregg.*
GEORGE CUNNINGHAM	*Alan Webb.*
LENA	*Moya Nugent.*
SIBYL HESTON	*Alison Leggatt.*
MICHAEL DOYLE	*Edward Underdown.*
A YOUNG MAN	*Anthony Pelissier.*
HODGE (Dresser)	*Kenneth Carten.*

TIME.—The Present.

SHADOW PLAY

SCENE I

The SCENE *is a well-furnished, rather luxurious bedroom in the Gayforths' house in Mayfair. There is a bed on the* L. *with a table by the side of it on which are various bottles, books and a telephone. Below the bed there is a door which leads to the bathroom. On the* R. *there is a door leading to the passage and the rest of the house. Above this is a dressing-table. At the foot of the bed there is a small sofa.*

When the CURTAIN *rises* LENA, VICTORIA (VICKY) GAY-FORTH'S *maid, is bustling about the room. It is about midnight and she is laying out a dressing-gown or negligée on the bed and generally arranging the room for the night.*

VICKY *and* MARTHA *come in from the* R. VICKY *is about thirty, beautifully gowned. Her manner is bored and irritable.* MARTHA *is slightly older, also well dressed but more tranquil.*

VICKY. . . . It couldn't matter less whether I go to Alice's or not—in fact it would be infinitely more comfortable for everybody concerned if I didn't.

MARTHA. What nonsense!

VICKY. Alice's parties are always dreadful, and I don't feel in the mood even for a good party to-night.

(*She slips off her cloak and* LENA *takes it.*)

MARTHA. What's the matter?

VICKY. I've told you—I've got a headache. (*She crosses to the dressing-table and sits.*)

MARTHA. I think you're unwise. (*She sits on the sofa.*)

VICKY. What do you mean, darling?

MARTHA. You know perfectly well what I mean.

VICKY. Of course I do, but I'm getting tired of everybody being subtle and hiding behind the furniture—I know that Simon will go without me and I know that Sibyl will be there and I know that if I don't go he will leave with her and if I do go he will leave with me and wish he was leaving with her. I also know that I'm bored stiff with the whole situation—let it rip——

MARTHA. Line of least resistance.

VICKY. Exactly—I have a headache—I feel thoroughly disagreeable—all I want is sleep—no more resisting—just sleep—— Lena—give me three Anytal——

LENA. Three, madame?

VICKY. Yes, three—and you can go to bed.

LENA. Yes, madame.

MARTHA. Is the extra tablet a gesture of defiance?

VICKY. Don't be tiresome, Martha.

(LENA *brings her three tablets from a bottle by the bed, and a glass of water.*)

MARTHA. Do you take those things every night?

VICKY (*swallowing the tablets*). No, darling, I don't. And even if I did it wouldn't matter a bit—they're perfectly harmless.

LENA. Are you sure that's all, madame?

VICKY. Yes, thank you, Lena—good night.

LENA. Good night, madame.

(*She goes out* R.)

MARTHA. I don't like seeing people unhappy.

VICKY. I'm not in the least unhappy—just tired. (*She rises and crosses* L.)

MARTHA. How much do you care?

VICKY. What do you mean, care?

(*She takes the dressing-gown off the bed and goes into the bathroom, leaving the door open.*)

MARTHA (*firmly*). About Simon and Sibyl.

VICKY. Heart-broken, dear—— (*She laughs.*) You mustn't be deceived by my gay frivolity, it's really only masking agony and defeat and despair——

MARTHA (*helping herself to a cigarette*). You're extremely annoying.

VICKY. That's what you wanted, isn't it?

MARTHA. You needn't be suspicious of me, you know —I have no axe to grind—I merely wanted to help——

VICKY. You're a noble, understanding old friend, darling, that's what you are, and I must say I should like to crack you over the head with a bottle.

MARTHA. Thank you, dear.

(*The telephone rings.*)

VICKY. Answer that, will you?—it's probably Michael—I'll be out in a minute——

MARTHA. All right. (*She goes to the telephone.*) Hallo—No, it's Martha—— She's in the bath-room, she'll be out in a minute—— No, she's not—— We've been to a play and it was so good that it gave her a headache—hold on, here she is——

(VICKY *comes in in a dressing-gown, flings herself on to the bed and takes the telephone.*)

VICKY. Hallo, Michael—— No, I'm not—— Yes, I've doped myself to the eyes and I'm about to go off into a coma—— Of course you can't, don't be so idiotic—what are you in such a state about?—I thought we'd settled all that——

(MARTHA *sits on the sofa again.*)

It's no use lowering your voice like that—Martha can hear perfectly well, she's got ears like a hawk——

MARTHA. Perhaps you'd like me to go?

VICKY (*to* MARTHA). Be quiet, darling—— (*At the telephone.*) I'm tired, Michael, and I've got a headache and so will you kindly shut up—— Yes, all right— to-morrow—— Good God, no, I shall be sound asleep—— Go away, Michael, I can't bear any more—— (*She hangs up.*) It's lovely being loved, isn't it? (*She rolls over on the bed face downwards.*)

MARTHA. You'd better get into bed—— (*She rises.*)

VICKY. Perhaps you'd like to fill a hot-water bottle and take my temperature?

MARTHA (*patiently*). Have you got a book to read?

VICKY. Yes, but it's unreadable.

MARTHA. Do get into bed.

VICKY. Shut up, and don't fuss——

MARTHA (*seriously*). I really wish I could do something——

VICKY (*violently*). Stop it, I tell you—I don't want your sympathy—I don't want anybody's sympathy—whatever happens, happens—let it—what does it matter——

MARTHA. Very well. (*She turns to go, picking up her cloak from the sofa.*)

VICKY (*jumping off the bed and running over to her*). I'm sorry—I know I'm beastly, but you see it's no use discussing things—the Anytal will begin to work soon and I shall have a nice long sleep and feel much better in the morning—— It was the play that upset me, I think—you were quite right—everybody seemed to be having such a good time, didn't they? (*She takes a cigarette, lights it and sits on the bed.*) It's a bit tantalizing to see everybody having quite such a good time—it would be so much easier if we had music when things go wrong—music and a little dancing and the certainty of "Happy ever after "—I hope you didn't miss the ironic twist at the end when they were married—crashing chords and complete tidiness—very convenient—— Go away, darling—go and collect George and Simon and go on to Alice's—I shall go to sleep in a minute—really I will—— (*She goes round and lies on the sofa.*)

MARTHA. All right—I'll telephone you in the morning——

(*She kisses her and is about to go, when* SIMON *comes into the room. He is wearing a dressing-gown over his evening clothes.*)

VICKY (*surprised*). Simon!

SIMON (*to* MARTHA). George is waiting for you, Martha—he's getting a bit restive.

VICKY. Aren't you going to Alice's?

SIMON. No, I didn't feel that I could face it.

VICKY. Oh, I see.

MARTHA. Do you want me to make excuses for you both, or just not say anything about it?

VICKY. Say that you haven't seen us, and why aren't we there, and is there any truth in the rumour that we're not getting on very well—— (*She laughs.*)

SIMON. Don't be silly, Vicky.

VICKY. Say that I've gone to Ostend with Michael and that Simon's shot himself—but only in the leg.

SIMON (*bitterly*). Say that it's perfectly true that we're not getting on very well—say that it's due to incompatibility of humour.

MARTHA (*crossing in front of him to the door* R.). I shall say that I don't know you at all--any more.

(*She goes out.*)

VICKY (*calling after her*). Give my love to Sibyl!

SIMON. That was a bit cheap, wasn't it?

VICKY. I thought it was only kind—Sibyl can't live without love—like the woman in the play to-night— don't you remember——? (*She hums.*) "Nobody can live without loving somebody, nobody can love without leaving somebody!"

SIMON. You mustn't forget to sing that to Michael. (*He crosses to the door* L.)

VICKY. Are we going to bicker? There's nothing like a nice bicker to round off a jolly evening.

SIMON. I'm getting a little tired of bickering.

VICKY. Let's not then, let's be absolutely divine to each other—let's pretend.

SIMON. I didn't go to Alice's party on purpose——

VICKY. I didn't think it was a sudden attack of amnesia.
SIMON. I want to talk to you.
VICKY. Do you, Simon? What about?
SIMON. Lots of things.
VICKY. Name fifteen.
SIMON. Seriously.
VICKY. There you are, you see—our moods are clashing again—it really is most unfortunate.
SIMON. I failed to notice during the evening that your spirits were so abnormally high. (*He sits on the bed.*)
VICKY. A sudden change for the better, dear, let's make the most of it.
SIMON. There's something I want to say to you—I've been wanting to say it for quite a while.
VICKY. Take the plunge, my darling—we're alone in the swimming-bath.
SIMON. Would you consider divorcing me?
VICKY. Oh, Simon!
SIMON. If I made everything easy——
VICKY. Naming Sibyl?
SIMON. Of course not.
VICKY. You mean you'd prefer to be implicated with a professional homebreaker as opposed to an amateur one?
SIMON. I would like, if possible, to keep this conversation impersonal.
VICKY. We might put on fancy dress for it.
SIMON. I'm serious, Vicky. (*He rises and crosses* R.)
VICKY. I'm told that all really funny comedians are serious.
SIMON. You haven't answered my question yet.
VICKY. I thought perhaps I hadn't heard it quite clearly.
SIMON. I want you to divorce me.
VICKY. Yes, now I hear—it's a beastly question, isn't it?
SIMON. Not so very beastly if you analyse it—quite sensible really.

VICKY. It oughtn't to be such a shock—but somehow it is—it makes me feel a little sick.

SIMON. I'm sorry.

VICKY (*swinging her feet off the sofa*). Don't worry about being sorry—feeling a little sick doesn't matter that much.

SIMON. I've thought it all over very carefully.

VICKY. Oh, Simon, have you? Have you really?

SIMON. Of course I have. It's been on my mind for a long time.

VICKY. How sinister that sounds—surely not for a very long time?

SIMON. Long enough.

VICKY. You're cruelly definite.

SIMON. It's less cruel to be definite—in the long run.

VICKY. It's been an awfully short run—really.

SIMON. You haven't answered me yet.

VICKY. An amicable divorce—everything below board?

SIMON. Yes.

VICKY. Where will you go with your temporary light of love? The South of France, or just good old Brighton?

SIMON. I don't think we need discuss that.

VICKY. It's a nasty business, isn't it—a very nasty business.

SIMON. Not necessarily, if it can be arranged discreetly and without fuss.

VICKY. Do you love her so much? Sybil I mean.

SIMON. I'd rather not discuss that either. (*He turns away and sits at the dressing-table.*)

VICKY. Perhaps you'd prefer to conduct the whole thing by signs—sort of Dumb Crambo.

SIMON. You're unbelievably irritating.

VICKY. When did you first begin to hate me?—When did I first begin to get on your nerves?—What did I say?—What did I do?—Was it a dress I wore—the way I laughed at somebody's joke?—Was I suddenly gay when you were sad?—Was I insensitive?—Was I
**

dull? When did it start—tell me if you can remember —please tell me.

SIMON. Don't be so foolish.

VICKY. I won't be irritating any more, Simon—I'll try to be sensible—really I will—but I must know why —why things change—I wish to God I hadn't taken those sleeping tablets—my head's going round—I would so love to be clear, just at this moment, but nothing's clear at all——

SIMON. I didn't know you'd taken anything. (*He rises and crosses to her.*)

VICKY. Don't be alarmed—I'm not becoming a drug fiend—it's an amiable, gentle prescription, just to make me sleep when I have a headache, or when I'm overtired or unhappy——

SIMON. There's the overture—we shall be late.

VICKY. What did you say?

SIMON. . . . You really ought not to get into the habit of taking things to make you sleep—however harmless they are——

VICKY. We've only been married five years—it seems longer at moments—then it seems no time at all——

(*The music begins, and, after a few chords, stops again.*)

SIMON. There it is again—listen.

VICKY. If you really love Sibyl, deeply and truly, it's different, but I have an awful feeling that you don't —anyhow, not enough——

SIMON. We will wander on together—
Through the sunny summer weather—
To our cosy little chateau
Like a pastoral by Watteau.

VICKY ⎫ (*together*). To our cosy little Chateau on the
SIMON ⎭ Rhine.

SIMON. . . . It isn't that I don't love you—I always shall love you—but this is something else—I don't know what started it, but I do know that it's terribly strong— and then there's Michael—I've been awfully angry about Michael——

VICKY. That's idiotic—Michael doesn't mean a thing to me—you know perfectly well he doesn't——

(*The music begins again, this time more loudly.*)

SIMON. There it is again—do hurry. (*He dances a few steps.*)

VICKY (*calling*). Lena—Lena—hurry up—I was miserable anyhow to-night—all the time we were in the theatre—everybody was having such a good time—and then they were married in the end—that was funny, wasn't it ?—about them being married in the end . . .

SIMON. . . . It isn't that I want to make you unhappy, but you must admit we haven't been hitting it off particularly well during the last year—if we're not comfortable together surely it would be much more sensible to separate——

(*The scene darkens. The side flats move off and up stage away from the centre flat.*)

VICKY. I feel so sad inside about it—I wish I could make you understand—it was so lovely in the beginning——

SIMON. Things never stay the same—you can't expect what was lovely then to be lovely now——

VICKY (*almost crying*). Why not—why not ?—Then we were happy——

SIMON. But, darling, you must see——

"THEN."

SIMON. Here in the light of this unkind familiar now
Every gesture is clear and cold for us,
Even yesterday's growing old for us,
   Everything changed somehow.
   If some forgotten lover's vow
Could make a memory in my heart again,
Perhaps the joys that we knew would start again.
   Can't we acclaim an hour or so
   The past is not so long ago.

VICKY. Then, love was complete for us,
Then, the days were sweet for us,

Life rose to its feet for us
  And stepped aside
  Before our pride.
Then, we knew the best of it,
Then, our hearts stood the test of it.
Now, the magic has flown,
We face the unknown
Apart and alone.

SIMON. Hodge—where's Hodge?—I must change—quick—we're going back.

(*The orchestra swells.* FLORRIE (LENA)—*comes hurrying in* R. *with an evening gown over her arm and a pair of shoes, a mirror, a powder-puff, etc., in her hands.* VICKY *sinks on to the bed.*)

You can't sit there—they're striking—we're going back——

FLORRIE. Here, dear—here's a chair.

VICKY. I'm not sure that I want to—I'm not at all sure—maybe it won't be as lovely as I think it was——

SIMON. Don't be such a fool—grab it while you can—grab every scrap of happiness while you can—Hodge—come on——

(HODGE, *a dresser, comes in with a dinner-jacket.* SIMON *takes off his dressing-gown and puts on the dinner-jacket.* VICKY *is changing on the opposite side of the stage. Meanwhile the whole scene is changing. The lights in the foreground fade except for the two spotlights on* SIMON *and* VICKY.)

VICKY (*breathlessly*). Play—go on playing—we must have music——

(SIMON *comes down to the footlights and begins to sing to the conductor. He sings a verse and chorus of* "*We Must Have Music.*")

"PLAY, ORCHESTRA, PLAY."

Listen to the strain it plays once more for us,
There it is again, the past in store for us.

Wake in memory some forgotten song
Driving us along
And make harmony again a last encore for us.

Play, orchestra, play,
Play something light and sweet and gay,
  For we must have music,
  We must have music
To drive our fears away.

While our illusions swiftly fade for us,
  Let's have an orchestra score.
In the confusions the years have made for us,
  Serenade for us, just once more.
Life needn't be grey,
Although it's changing day by day,
Though a few old dreams may decay,
Play, orchestra, play.

(VICKY *joins him and they finish it together. Meanwhile all the lights fade entirely except for two pin spots on the two of them. The spot on* SIMON *goes out and* VICKY *is left singing almost hysterically* "We Must Have Music." *The orchestra rises to a crescendo and there is a complete black-out.*)

(*To measured music and in a pool of light,* SIBYL HESTON *appears. She lights a cigarette and glances at her wrist-watch.* SIMON *appears from the opposite side of the stage. He stands a little apart from her. The music stops.*)

SIBYL. I'm waiting—I'm waiting—why don't you tell her?

SIMON. It will hurt her, you know.

SIBYL. She can weep on Michael's shoulder—it's a very attractive shoulder.

SIMON. I don't want to hurt her.

SIBYL. She'll have to know sooner or later. Nobody can live without loving somebody, nobody can love without leaving somebody.

SIMON. I saw you in the theatre to-night—you looked marvellous.

SIBYL. Sweet Simon.
SIMON. Very cool and green and wise.
SIBYL. Not wise—— Oh, my dear, not wise at all. I happen to love you.
SIMON. Is that so unwise?
SIBYL. Let's say—indefinite!
SIMON. It's less cruel to be indefinite in the long run.
SIBYL. Tell her the truth—you must tell her the truth.
SIMON. I have been awfully angry about Michael.
SIBYL. Why be angry, darling? It's such waste of energy.
SIMON. I don't like Vicky making a fool of herself.
SIBYL. I don't like Vicky making a fool of you.
SIMON. I didn't know she took things to make her sleep.
SIBYL. You must tell her the truth—sleep or no sleep.

(*The music starts again.* MICHAEL *walks on. He passes* SIBYL *and* SIMON, *stops, lights a cigarette and glances at his wrist-watch. The music stops.*)

MICHAEL. I'm waiting—I'm waiting—why don't you tell her?
SIMON. I don't want to hurt her.
MICHAEL. Give her my love.
SIMON. That was a bit cheap, wasn't it?
SIBYL (*laughing*). When did she first begin to get on your nerves, Simon? What started it? Was it a dress she wore? Was it the way she laughed at somebody's joke? Was she suddenly gay when you were sad? Was she insensitive? Was she dull?
MICHAEL. Was she dull?
SIBYL. Was she dull?
SIMON. It was so lovely in the beginning.
SIBYL. Things never stay the same—you can't expect what was lovely then to be lovely now.
SIMON. We're going back all the same—it's our only chance——
SIBYL. Was she dull?

MICHAEL. Was she dull?

SIMON. Shut up—shut up both of you—we're going back——

(*He begins to sing, and as he sings the lights fade on* SIBYL *and* MICHAEL.)

Life needn't be grey
Though it is changing day by day.
Though a few old dreams may decay
Play Orchestra—Play Orchestra—Play Orchestra—Play——

BLACK OUT.

SCENE II

The lights come up on a moonlit garden. There is a stone seat on the R. *of the stage.* VICKY *and a* YOUNG MAN *are sitting on it.*

(*See Photograph of Scene.*)

VICKY. It's nice and cool in the garden.

YOUNG MAN. It's nice and cool in the garden.

VICKY. Country-house dances can be lovely when the weather's good, can't they?

YOUNG MAN. Rather—rather—yes, of course—rather.

VICKY. I'm waiting for something.

YOUNG MAN. Country-house dances can be lovely when the weather's good, can't they?

VICKY. This is where it all began.

YOUNG MAN. It's nice and cool in the garden.

VICKY. Please hurry, my darling, I can't wait to see you for the first time.

YOUNG MAN. Do you know this part of the country?

VICKY. Intimately. I'm staying here with my aunt, you know.

YOUNG MAN. Does she ride to hounds?

VICKY. Incessantly.

YOUNG MAN. That's ripping, isn't it?—I mean it really is ripping.

VICKY. Yes. She's a big woman and she kills little foxes—she's kind and fond, but she dearly loves killing little foxes.

YOUNG MAN. We're getting on awfully well—it's awfully nice out here—I think you're awfully pretty.

VICKY. This is waste of time—he should be here by now—walking through the trees—coming towards me.

YOUNG MAN. I think you're an absolute fizzer.

VICKY. Yes, I remember you saying that—it made me want to giggle—but I controlled myself beautifully.

YOUNG MAN. I think you know my sister—she's in pink.

VICKY. I remember her clearly—a beastly girl.

YOUNG MAN. In pink.

VICKY (*suddenly*). In pink—in pink—
Your sister's dressed in pink;
It wasn't very wise I think
To choose that unbecoming shade
Of pink——

YOUNG MAN. I'm so glad you like her—you must come and stay with us—My mother's an absolute fizzer—you'd love her.

VICKY. God forbid!

YOUNG MAN. That's absolutely ripping of you.

VICKY. Now—now—at last—you're walking through the trees—hurry——

(SIMON *comes through the trees* c. *He is smoking a cigarette.*)

I thought you'd missed your entrance.

SIMON. Are you engaged for this dance?

VICKY. I was, but I'll cut it if you'll promise to love me always and never let anything or anybody spoil it—never——

SIMON. But of course—that's understood.

YOUNG MAN. Will you excuse me—I have to dance with Lady Dukes.

VICKY. Certainly.

YOUNG MAN. Good hunting.
VICKY. Thank you so much—it's been so boring.
YOUNG MAN. Not at all—later perhaps.

(*He goes*, R.)

SIMON. Well—here we are.
VICKY. The first time—we knew at once, didn't we? Don't you remember how we discussed it afterwards?
SIMON. I saw you in the ballroom—I wondered who you were.
VICKY. My name's Victoria—Victoria Marden.
SIMON. Mine's Simon Gayforth.
VICKY. How do you do?
SIMON. Quite well, thank you.
VICKY. I suppose you came down from London for the dance?
SIMON. Yes, I'm staying with the Bursbys——
VICKY. What do you do?
SIMON. I'm in a bank.
VICKY. High up in the bank? Or just sitting in a cage totting up things?
SIMON. Oh, quite high up really—it's a very good bank.
VICKY. I'm so glad.
SIMON. How lovely you are.
VICKY. No, no, that came later—you've skipped some.
SIMON. Sorry.
VICKY. You're nice and thin—your eyes are funny—you move easily—I'm afraid you're terribly attractive——
SIMON. You never said that.
VICKY. No, but I thought it.
SIMON. Stick to the script.
VICKY. Small talk—a lot of small talk with quite different thoughts going on behind it—this garden's really beautiful—are you good at gardens?
SIMON. No, but I'm persevering—I'm all right on the more straightforward blooms—you know—Snap-

dragons, Sweet William, Cornflowers and Tobacco plant —and I can tell a Dorothy Perkins a mile off.

VICKY. That hedge over there is called Cupressus Macrocapa.

SIMON. Do you swear it?

VICKY. It grows terrifically quickly, but they do say that it goes a bit thin underneath in about twenty years——

SIMON. How beastly of them to say that—it's slander.

VICKY. Did you know about Valerian smelling of cats?

SIMON. You're showing off again.

VICKY. It's true.

SIMON. I can go one better than that—Lotuses smell of pineapple.

VICKY (*sadly*). Everything smells of something else—it's dreadfully confusing——

SIMON. Never mind, darling—I love you desperately—I knew it the first second I saw you——

VICKY. You're skipping again.

(*They sing a light Duet: " You Were There," after which they dance.*)

"YOU WERE THERE."

1.

SIMON. Was it in the real world or was I in a dream?
Was it just a note from some eternal theme?
Was it accidental or accurately planned?
How could I hesitate
Knowing that my fate
Led me by the hand?
You were there.
I saw you and my heart stopped beating,
You were there,
And in that first enchanting meeting
Life changed its tune, the stars, the moon came near
to me.

Dreams that I dreamed, like magic seemed to be near
to me, dear to me.
You were there.
Your eyes looked into mine and faltered.
Everywhere
The colour of the whole world altered.
False became true,
My universe tumbled in two,
The earth became heaven, for you were there.
VICKY. How can we explain it—the spark, and then
the fire?
How add up the total of our heart's desire?
Maybe some magician, a thousand years ago—
Wove us a subtle spell—so that we could know—so that
we could tell—
You were there—(*etc.*)

(*During the dance the lights fade on the scene and they finish in each other's arms in a spotlight. The spotlight fades and in the darkness a voice is heard singing* "Then they knew the best of it—then their hearts stood the test of it," *etc.*

A spotlight picks up LENA—*singing, holding the tablets and a glass of water. After song fade again.*)

SCENE III

The lights go up again on the interior of a limousine.
MARTHA *and* GEORGE CUNNINGHAM *are sitting in it.*

GEORGE. On the whole this has been one of the most uncomfortable evenings I've ever spent.

MARTHA. There, there, dear, I know, but for heaven's sake don't go on about it.

GEORGE (*petulantly*). Why, if they had to take us to dinner and a play, should they have chosen that particular dinner and that particular play?

MARTHA. What was wrong with the dinner?

GEORGE. Gastronomically speaking it was excellent, but the atmosphere reeked with conjugal infelicity—when people are at loggerheads they should refrain from entertaining—it's bad for the digestive tract.

MARTHA. For an elderly barrister you're unduly sensitive.

GEORGE. I expected the grouse to sit up on its plate and offer me a brief.

MARTHA. Never mind, when we get to Alice's you'll be able to have a nice drink and talk to some lovely young things and feel much better.

GEORGE. And why that play? Sentimental twaddle.

MARTHA. The music was lovely.

GEORGE. That's no good to me. You know perfectly well I can't distinguish " Abide with me " from " God Save the King."

MARTHA. Concentrate on " God Save the King."

GEORGE. I couldn't even go to sleep with those idiotic people loving each other for ever all over the stage.

MARTHA. Well, we'll go to a nice soothing gangster picture to-morrow night and you can watch people killing each other all over the screen.

GEORGE. What's wrong with them, anyway?

MARTHA. Who, Simon and Vicky?

GEORGE. Yes.

MARTHA. They're unhappy.

GEORGE. Well, they oughtn't to be—they've got everything they want.

MARTHA. Sibyl Heston's got hold of Simon and Vicky's trying to pretend that she doesn't mind a bit and everything's in a dreary muddle—women like Sibyl Heston ought to be shot.

GEORGE. Sometimes they are.

MARTHA. Not often enough.

GEORGE. I suppose Vicky's got a young man hanging around, hasn't she?

MARTHA. No, not really—she's been encouraging Michael Doyle a bit, but it doesn't mean anything—it's just part of the pretending.

GEORGE. Damn fools—they're all damn fools——

(VICKY *runs on from the side of the stage. She is picked up by a blue spotlight.*)

VICKY. Go away, you're spoiling it all—I know what you're saying—I know what everybody's saying——

MARTHA. I was only trying to help.

VICKY. I know—I know—you're very kind—but it isn't any use——

GEORGE. People were so much more sensible twenty years ago—take my sister, for instance—look how brilliantly she managed her life—you ought to have known my sister——

VICKY. In pink.

GEORGE. In brilliant pink.

VICKY (*singing*). In pink—in pink
Your sister's dressed in pink,
It wasn't very wise I think
To choose that unbecoming shade
Of pink——!

(SIMON *enters and is picked up in a blue spot.*)

SIMON. This compartment is reserved—we're going back.

GEORGE. I'm most awfully sorry.

VICKY. There are probably some empty ones farther along the train.

MARTHA. But of course—we quite understand—George, help me with my dressing-case——

SIMON. Allow me——

(*He helps them to remove imaginary luggage from the rack.*)

GEORGE. I suppose you don't happen to know what time we reach Milan?

SIMON. I know we arrive in Venice at about six-thirty—I think there's about four hours' difference.

VICKY. It's really charming of you to be so considerate—you see we are on our honeymoon.

MARTHA. Grab every scrap of happiness while you can.

GEORGE. We shall meet later.
SIMON. I hope so.

(MARTHA *and* GEORGE *step out of the car and walk off.* SIMON *and* VICKY *climb in. The spotlights follow them into the cab.*)

Well, here we are.
VICKY. My name's Victoria.
SIMON. Victoria what?
VICKY. Victoria Gayforth.
SIMON. What a silly name.
VICKY. I adore it.
SIMON. That's because you're sentimental.
VICKY. Fiercely sentimental—over romantic, too.
SIMON. Dearest darling.
VICKY. The wedding went off beautifully, didn't it?
SIMON. Brief, to the point, and not unduly musical.
VICKY. Didn't Mother look nice?
SIMON. Not particularly.
VICKY. Oh, Simon!
SIMON. It was her hat, I think—it looked as though it were in a hurry and couldn't stay very long.
VICKY. Was that man who slapped you on the back your uncle?
SIMON. Yes, dear—that was my uncle.
VICKY. I'm so sorry.
SIMON. He ran away to sea, you know, when he was very young, and then, unfortunately, he ran back again.
VICKY. Your sister looked charming.
SIMON. In pink.
VICKY. In pink—In pink——
SIMON. Stop it—stop it—you'll wake yourself up.
VICKY. It was that rhyme in the play to-night—it keeps coming into my mind.
SIMON. Do concentrate—we're on our honeymoon.
VICKY. Happy ever after.
SIMON. That's right.
VICKY. Do you think that those people we turned

out of the carriage ever loved each other as much as we do?

SIMON. Nobody ever loved each other as much as we do, with the possible exception of Romeo and Juliet, Heloise and Abelard, Paolo and Francesca, Dante and Beatrice——

VICKY. I wish she hadn't been called Beatrice—it's such a smug name.

SIMON. Anthony and Cleopatra, Pelleas and Melisande——

VICKY. I've always felt that Melisande was rather a silly girl—so vague.

SIMON. All right—wash out Melisande.

VICKY (*looking out of the window*). Look at all those little houses flashing by—think of all the millions of people living in them—eating and drinking—dressing and undressing—getting up and going to bed—having babies——

SIMON. When I was a young bride I never mentioned such things on my honeymoon.

VICKY. Things never stay the same.

SIMON. It was considered immodest to do anything but weep gently and ask for glasses of water.

VICKY. I'm abandoned, darling—I can't wait to be in your arms——

SIMON. Dear heart—— (*He takes her in his arms.*)

VICKY (*struggling*). No, no—this isn't right—my clothes are all wrong—I must go——

SIMON. Don't go.

VICKY. I must—this dressing-gown's all wrong I tell you—when we arrived in Venice I was wearing a blue tailor made—and then later we dined—and I was in grey——

SIMON. In grey—in grey—
Your dress was soft and grey.
It seems a million years away,
The ending of that sweet and happy day.

VICKY. Oh, darling——
SIMON. Don't go——
VICKY. I must—I must——

(*She steps out of the carriage and disappears into the darkness.* SIMON, *left alone, sings a reprise of "You Were There," and the lights fade completely.*)

SCENE IV

When the lights go up SIMON *and* VICKY *are sitting at a little table with a shaded light on it. They are just finishing dinner.*
(*See Photograph of Scene.*)

SIMON. We can sit on the piazza for a little and then we can drift . . .

VICKY. Let's call the gondola right away and cut out the piazza—I'm a big drifting girl.

SIMON. I think the band on the piazza will be awfully disappointed.

VICKY. It's funny, isn't it, to be so frightfully in love that you feel as if you were going mad?

SIMON. Ever so funny.

VICKY. Do you think our front gondolier is nicer than our back one?

SIMON. Not altogether—he has better teeth, of course, but then he's about fifty years younger.

VICKY. Let's come here again in fifty years' time.

SIMON. All right.

VICKY. We can arrange to be carried on to the train —it will be quite simple.

SIMON. It won't be a train, darling—it will be a pointed silver bullet leaving Croydon at four and arriving here at twenty-past three.

VICKY. Oh dear!

SIMON. What's the matter?

VICKY. We haven't quarrelled yet.

SIMON. Never mind.

VICKY. We'll have a nice quarrel when we get back to London, won't we?

SIMON. I shall sulk for the first few days, anyhow— I'm the sulky type, you know.

VICKY. That's why I married you.

SIMON. Oh, darling—I'm going to be terribly serious for a minute—will you bear with me?
VICKY. Of course.
SIMON. There's something I want to say to you—I've been wanting to say it for quite a while——
VICKY (*with panic in her voice*). Oh, Simon, don't—what is it? What is it?
SIMON. I love you.
VICKY (*putting her head down on the table*). You mustn't make people cry on their honeymoon—it's not cricket.
SIMON (*tenderly*). Dearest—everything's cricket if only you have faith.
VICKY. When did you know you loved me—the very first minute, I mean?
SIMON. In the garden—during the dance—I saw you and my heart stopped beating——
VICKY. It was a most enchanted meeting.
SIMON. Life changed its tune—the stars and moon came near to me——
VICKY. Dreams that I'd dreamed, like magic seemed to be clear to me—dear to me——
SIMON. False became true—my universe tumbled in two—the earth became heaven—for you were there——
VICKY. Stop it—stop it—it's that damned musical comedy again—going round and round in my head—listen—before the dream breaks say what you said that night in Venice—say it from your heart as you said it then—say it, please—please——
SIMON. I'm not sure that I can remember—it's a long while ago——
VICKY. Please, Simon—please——
SIMON. It's this, darling—we're here together close as close and it's the beginning—but we're going to be together for a long time—probably all our lives, so we must be careful—I want to reassure you now about later on—about any tricks the future might play on us —I know I love you with all my heart—with every bit of me—it's easy now, because it's summer weather and there isn't a cloud in the sky and we're alone—but there'll

be other people presently—we can't live our whole lives on this little island—other people are dangerous. They spoil true love, not consciously because they want to, but because they're themselves—out for all they can get—mischievous—you do see what I mean, don't you——?

VICKY. You mean they might make us want them one day instead of each other.

SIMON. Yes, but only a little—not like this—not all the way round——

VICKY. I can't imagine even that—I'm very single tracked.

SIMON. Don't look sad—don't even have a flicker of unhappiness, not for ages yet, anyway—but whenever you do—if I'm bad or foolish or unkind, or even unfaithful—just remember this, because this is what really matters—this lovely understanding of each other—it may be a jumping-off place for many future journeys—but however long the journey one's got to come back some time, and this is the white cliffs of Dover—hang on to the white cliffs of Dover——

VICKY. I'll try——

(*They hold hands for a moment across the table.*)

(*There is a burst of music which dies away on a discord. Then a dance tune starts and keeps up a steady rhythm during the ensuing scene. The light on* SIMON *and* VICKY *fades a little. They are sitting quite still gazing at each other.* SIBYL HESTON *and* MICHAEL DOYLE *dance on together out of the shadows. They are in a brilliant spotlight.*)

MICHAEL. We're a bit early, aren't we? They're still on their honeymoon.

SIBYL. Nonsense. The curtain will be lowered between scenes two and three to denote a lapse of four years—

(*The light on* SIMON *and* VICKY *goes out completely*)

MICHAEL (*over his shoulder*). I'm so sorry.

SIBYL. It's impossible to dance here.

MICHAEL. They put so many tables on the floor.
SIBYL. There's no room at all.
MICHAEL. Let's go on to the Florida.
SIBYL. And the Cocoanut Grove.
MICHAEL. And the Four Hundred.
SIBYL. And the Blue Train.

(SIMON *and* VICKY *dance on in another spotlight.*)

SIMON. There's always the Florida.
VICKY. And the Cocoanut Grove.
SIMON. And the Four Hundred.
VICKY. And the Blue Train.

(*The rhythm gets slightly faster. The two couples circle round each other.*)

SIBYL. The Florida.
SIMON. The Cocoanut Grove.
MICHAEL. The Four Hundred.
VICKY. The Blue Train.
SIBYL. The Florida.
VICKY. The Cocoanut Grove.
MICHAEL. The Four Hundred.
SIMON. The Blue Train.

The music gets faster still. They change partners. SIMON *dances with* SIBYL *and* MICHAEL *with* VICKY—*then they change back to each other again—then once more—all saying together:* "The Florida," "The Cocoanut Grove," "The Four Hundred," "The Blue Train." MICHAEL *and* VICKY *disappear and* SIBYL *and* SIMON *are left dancing round and round together, faster and faster. From the darkness can be heard voices shouting rhythmically:* "The Florida," "The Cocoanut Grove," "The Four Hundred," "The Blue Train," *coming to a crescendo, and then a*

BLACK OUT.

SCENE V

LENA *appears on the right-hand side of the stage with a telephone.* MARTHA *appears on the opposite side, also with a telephone. Both in spotlights.*

MARTHA. Hallo—who is it?
LENA. It's Lena, madame.
MARTHA. Oh, Lena—yes—what is it?
LENA. Mr. Gayforth asked me to telephone to you, madame——
MARTHA. Is anything wrong?
LENA. It's Mrs. Gayforth, madame—those sleeping tablets—Mr. Gayforth wants to know if you can leave the party and come at once——
MARTHA. Good heavens! Is she ill?
LENA. Yes, madame—that is—she's not exactly ill, but——
MARTHA. Have you sent for a doctor?
LENA. No, madame—Mr. Gayforth didn't want to send for a doctor until he'd seen you.
MARTHA. I'll come at once.
LENA. It was that extra Anytal tablet, madame—I knew she shouldn't have taken it——
MARTHA. I'll be there in a few minutes—in the meantime—give her some strong black coffee——

(*The lights fade. In the darkness* VICKY'S *voice is heard.*)

VICKY. Simon, Simon—where are you?—I'm lonely—I'm frightened—Don't go away from me yet—in spite of what they say there is still time if only we're careful——
SIMON. There's something I want to say to you—I've been wanting to say it for quite a while——
VICKY. Don't say it—don't say it yet.
SIMON. I would like, if possible, to keep this conversation impersonal.
VICKY. I would so love to be clear at this moment. But nothing's clear at all——

SIMON. I didn't know you had taken anything——
VICKY. It was only to make me sleep—whenever I'm tired or unhappy. Oh, Simon—Simon—come back—the White Cliffs of Dover—I'm trying so hard—I'm trying to hold on—don't leave me—don't leave me——

(*The lights are about to come up on the original opening bedroom scene.*)

SIMON. Give her a little more, Lena.
LENA. Yes, sir.
SIMON. You don't think we ought to send for a doctor?
MARTHA. No, she'll be all right.
SIMON. It was awfully sweet of you to come back, Martha—I got in a panic—you were the only one I could think of——
VICKY. I shall be sick if I have any more of that damned coffee.
SIMON. That's a very good idea—be sick.
VICKY. No, no—I hate being sick—it's mortifying—I'm perfectly all right now—really I am.

(*The lights slowly go up on the bedroom.* VICKY *is sitting on the edge of the bed.* SIMON *is sitting by her side with one arm round her, holding a cup of coffee in his other hand.* MARTHA *is kneeling on the floor at her feet.* LENA *is standing anxiously at the foot of the bed holding a coffee-pot.*)

SIMON. There, darling—won't you lie down a bit?
VICKY. Don't fuss.
SIMON. You ought to be ashamed of yourself.
VICKY. What are you rolling about on the floor for, Martha? It looks very silly.
MARTHA (*rising*). You may well ask.
VICKY. I think I should like a cigarette.
SIMON. Then you will be sick.
VICKY. No, it's passed off.
LENA (*handing her a cigarette*). Here, madame.
VICKY. Thank you, Lena. Match, please.
SIMON. Here, Martha, take this cup, will you?

(*He gives* MARTHA *the coffee-cup and lights* VICKY'S *cigarette.*)

VICKY. That's lovely. (*She puffs.*)
SIMON. It's all right, Lena—you can go to bed again.
LENA. Are you sure, sir?
SIMON. Yes, thank you, Lena.
LENA. Good night, sir.
SIMON. Good night.

(LENA *goes out* R.)

VICKY. Now perhaps somebody will explain. What happened to me?
SIMON. You just went mad, that's all—raving.
VICKY (*interested*). Did I froth at the mouth?
SIMON. I don't know—I was too agitated to notice.
MARTHA. I think I'd better go back to Alice's.
VICKY. Alice's! Oh yes, of course. Oh, Simon—I remember now.
SIMON. Don't think of anything—just relax.
MARTHA (*kissing her*). Good night, darling.
VICKY (*absently—her thoughts a long way away*). Good night.
MARTHA. Good night, Simon.
SIMON. Thanks awfully, Martha.

(MARTHA *goes out.*)

VICKY. I'm so sorry, Simon—I'm feeling quite tranquil now—let's talk about the divorce in the morning.
SIMON. Divorce? What do you mean?
VICKY. You asked me to divorce you, didn't you?
SIMON. Certainly not.
VICKY. Are you trying to make me believe that that was part of the dream?
SIMON. I don't know what you're talking about.
VICKY. It's sweet of you to lie—but it won't wash.

(SIMON *sits on the bed again and puts his arms round her.*)

SIMON. Please forgive me.

VICKY (*sleepily*). We'll talk it all over calmly—to-morrow.

SIMON. All right.

VICKY (*resting her head on his shoulder*). If you really love her all that much I'll try not to be beastly about it——

SIMON. I don't love anybody that much.

VICKY. What did I do when I went mad? I'm so interested.

SIMON. You talked a lot—I thought it was nonsense at first and then I realized that it was true—then you began dancing about the room—then you really did go mad—and I got very frightened and told Lena to ring up Martha——

VICKY. It was certainly a very strange feeling——

(*She closes her eyes and the music starts again very softly.*)

SIMON. It will be all right now—it really will—I promise.

VICKY. The music's beginning again.

The music swells. SIMON *lifts her gently on to the bed and covers her over with the counterpane. Then he kisses her, disentangles her cigarette from her fingers, tiptoes across the room and switches off the lights, all but a little lamp by the bed, and stretches himself on the sofa at her feet.*

The music reaches a crescendo as——

The CURTAIN *falls.*

PROPERTY AND FURNITURE PLOT

As used at the Phœnix Theatre

Scene I

White sheepskin rug.
White and flowered pelmet and draperies to centre back and over bed.
1. Dressing-table with cover, 3-fold mirror, hand mirror, toilet brush, clothes brush, 2 scent sprays, brown ashtray.
2. White stool.
3. Round white table with white telephone, French novel, box of matches, glass match-stand, green ashtray, tumbler of water, bottle of aspirins.
4. Bed with cover, mattress, 2 pillows, 2 sheets, counterpane (net), blanket.
5. White sofa.

Bentwood chair off R. to go on stage.
Off L.
  Chair and mirror (for quick change).
  Garden furniture behind back flats.

Scene II

1. Stone seat.
2 and 3. Stone vases with large prop lilies.
4 and 5. Single steps.
Off R.
  Box with floor gloss.

Scene III

Taxi set behind blacks.
Off R.
  Glass of water, large bottle aspirins.

Scene IV

Blue curtains on black rods behind openings L.
1. Wicker table (doubled "We Were Dancing") with 2 coffee-cups and saucers wired on (*no* spoons).
2 and 3. Green and white armchairs.
4 and 5. Small vases of lilies.

Scene V

Front cloth. Nil. Megaphones for Company. Set Scene I as before.
Coffee-cup and saucer (Simon).

FURNITURE

Bed, made up with—
Mattress, 2 silk sheets.
Blanket, 2 pillows in silk cases.
Hangings—net.
Net bedcover.
Bedside table.
Dressing-table and mirror.
Dressing-table stool.
Thin short couch.
White fur carpet.
Pelmet.
Curtains.
Net curtains.
Dressing-table hangings.

Off R.
  Bentwood chair.
  Garden seat.
  2 stone edgings.
  2 stone urns.
  Taxi.
  2 green wood armchairs.
  Wicker table (double "We Were Dancing").
  2 coffee-cups wired to it.
  Green curtains on rods.
  Box with floor gloss.
  2 collapsible quick change rooms.

PROPERTIES

On Bed Table.
  French novel.
  Glass of water.
  Bottle of aspirin.
  Ashtray.
  Enamel cigarette-box.
  Club matches.
  Matches.
  Coffee-cup and saucer (last Scene).

On Dressing-Table.
  2 scent bottles.
  Dressing-table set (wired to table).
  Matches.
  Ashtray.
  Tin triple mirror.
  2 large lilies in large urns.
  2 small lilies in small urns.

Off R.
  Large bottle of aspirin.
  Glass of water.
  9 megaphones.

SKIN DEEP
Jon Lonoff

Comedy / 2m, 2f / Interior Unit Set

In *Skin Deep*, a large, lovable, lonely-heart, named Maureen Mulligan, gives romance one last shot on a blind-date with sweet awkward Joseph Spinelli; she's learned to pepper her speech with jokes to hide insecurities about her weight and appearance, while he's almost dangerously forthright, saying everything that comes to his mind. They both know they're perfect for each other, and in time they come to admit it.

They were set up on the date by Maureen's sister Sheila and her husband Squire, who are having problems of their own: Sheila undergoes a non-stop series of cosmetic surgeries to hang onto the attractive and much-desired Squire, who may or may not have long ago held designs on Maureen, who introduced him to Sheila. With Maureen particularly vulnerable to both hurting and being hurt, the time is ripe for all these unspoken issues to bubble to the surface.

"Warm-hearted comedy ... the laughter was literally show-stopping. A winning play, with enough good-humored laughs and sentiment to keep you smiling from beginning to end."
- TalkinBroadway.com

"It's a little Paddy Chayefsky, a lot Neil Simon and a quick-witted, intelligent voyage into the not-so-tranquil seas of middle-aged love and dating. The dialogue is crackling and hilarious; the plot simple but well-turned; the characters endearing and quirky; and lurking beneath the merriment is so much heartache that you'll stand up and cheer when the unlikely couple makes it to the inevitable final clinch."
- NYTheatreWorld.Com

SAMUELFRENCH.COM

COCKEYED
William Missouri Downs

Comedy / 3m, 1f / Unit Set

Phil, an average nice guy, is madly in love with the beautiful Sophia. The only problem is that she's unaware of his existence. He tries to introduce himself but she looks right through him. When Phil discovers Sophia has a glass eye, he thinks that might be the problem, but soon realizes that she really can't see him. Perhaps he is caught in a philosophical hyperspace or dualistic reality or perhaps beautiful women are just unaware of nice guys. Armed only with a B.A. in philosophy, Phil sets out to prove his existence and win Sophia's heart. This fast moving farce is the winner of the HotCity Theatre's GreenHouse New Play Festival. The St. Louis Post-Dispatch called Cockeyed a clever romantic comedy, Talkin' Broadway called it "hilarious," while Playback Magazine said that it was "fresh and invigorating."

Winner!
of the HotCity Theatre GreenHouse New Play Festival

"Rocking with laughter...hilarious...polished and engaging work draws heavily on the age-old conventions of farce: improbable situations, exaggerated characters, amazing coincidences, absurd misunderstandings, people hiding in closets and barely missing each other as they run in and out of doors...full of comic momentum as Cockeyed hurtles toward its conclusion."
- Talkin' Broadway

THE OFFICE PLAYS
Two full length plays by Adam Bock

THE RECEPTIONIST
Comedy / 2m., 2f. Interior

At the start of a typical day in the Northeast Office, Beverly deals effortlessly with ringing phones and her colleague's romantic troubles. But the appearance of a charming rep from the Central Office disrupts the friendly routine. And as the true nature of the company's business becomes apparent, The Receptionist raises disquieting, provocative questions about the consequences of complicity with evil.

"...Mr. Bock's poisoned Post-it note of a play."
- New York Times

"Bock's intense initial focus on the routine goes to the heart of *The Receptionist's* pointed, painfully timely allegory... elliptical, provocative play..."
- Time Out New York

THE THUGS
Comedy / 2m, 6f / Interior

The Obie Award winning dark comedy about work, thunder and the mysterious things that are happening on the 9th floor of a big law firm. When a group of temps try to discover the secrets that lurk in the hidden crevices of their workplace, they realize they would rather believe in gossip and rumors than face dangerous realities.

"Bock starts you off giggling, but leaves you with a chill."
- Time Out New York

"... a delightfully paranoid little nightmare that is both more chillingly realistic and pointedly absurd than anything John Grisham ever dreamed up."
- New York Times

SAMUELFRENCH.COM

NO SEX PLEASE, WE'RE BRITISH
Anthony Marriott and Alistair Foot

Farce / 7 m., 3 f. / Int.

A young bride who lives above a bank with her husband who is the assistant manager, innocently sends a mail order off for some Scandinavian glassware. What comes is Scandinavian pornography. The plot revolves around what is to be done with the veritable floods of pornography, photographs, books, films and eventually girls that threaten to engulf this happy couple. The matter is considerably complicated by the man's mother, his boss, a visiting bank inspector, a police superintendent and a muddled friend who does everything wrong in his reluctant efforts to set everything right, all of which works up to a hilarious ending of closed or slamming doors. This farce ran in London over eight years and also delighted Broadway audiences.

"Titillating and topical."
- "NBC TV"

"A really funny Broadway show."
- "ABC TV"

This work is published by Samuel French, an imprint of Concord Theatricals Corp.

No one shall make any changes in this title(s) for the purpose of production. No part of this book may be reproduced, stored in a retrieval system, scanned, uploaded, or transmitted in any form, by any means, now known or yet to be invented, including mechanical, electronic, digital, photocopying, recording, videotaping, or otherwise, without the prior written permission of the publisher. No one shall share this title(s), or any part of this title(s), through any social media or file hosting websites.

For all inquiries regarding motion picture, television, online/digital and other media rights, please contact Concord Theatricals Corp.

MUSIC AND THIRD-PARTY MATERIALS USE NOTE

Licensees are solely responsible for obtaining formal written permission from copyright owners to use copyrighted music and/or other copyrighted third-party materials (e.g. artworks, logos) in the performance of this play and are strongly cautioned to do so. If no such permission is obtained by the licensee, then the licensee must use only original music and materials that the licensee owns and controls. Licensees are solely responsible and liable for clearances of all third-party copyrighted materials, including without limitation music, and shall indemnify the copyright owners of the play(s) and their licensing agent, Concord Theatricals Corp., against any costs, expenses, losses and liabilities arising from the use of such copyrighted third-party materials by licensees. For music, please contact the appropriate music licensing authority in your territory for the rights to any incidental music.

IMPORTANT BILLING AND CREDIT REQUIREMENTS

If you have obtained performance rights to this title, please refer to your licensing agreement for important billing and credit requirements.

www.ingramcontent.com/pod-product-compliance
Lightning Source LLC
Chambersburg PA
CBHW070651300426
44111CB00013B/2362